IN THE ANIMAL KINGDOM

REPTILES HAVE SCALY SKIN

By Sarah Ridley

WAYLAND

www.waylandbooks.co.uk

First published in Great Britain in 2018
by Wayland

Copyright © Hodder and Stoughton, 2018

Editor: Sarah Peutrill
Designer: Lisa Peacock

ISBN: 978 1 5263 0930 3

Printed and bound in China

Wayland, an imprint of
Hachette Children's Group
Part of Hodder and Stoughton
Carmelite House
50 Victoria Embankment
London EC4Y 0DZ
An Hachette UK Company
www.hachette.co.uk
www.hachettechildrens.co.uk

Every attempt has been made to clear
copyright. Should there be any
inadvertent omission please apply to the
publisher for rectification.

Picture credits: Artrush/Shutterstock: 20. Ryan M Bolton/Shutterstock: 17b. Chantelle Bosch/Shutterstock: 12. Rainer von Brandis/istockphoto: 16. Jan Bures/Shutterstock: 6. Rich Carey/Shutterstock: 2b, 9b. Stephen Dalton/Nature PL: 15t. Davdeka/Shutterstock: 1, 9t. geoffsp/istockphoto: 10. Christian Ghimpe/Shutterstock: 7b. Ross Gordon Henry/Shutterstock: 23b. Alex Hyde/Nature PL: 13b. Eric Isselee/Shutterstock: 8b. Mark Kostich/istockphoto: 14. Brian E Kushner/Shutterstock: 13t. Tim Large-USA/Alamy: 8t. Mark MacEwan/Nature PL: 18, 19t. milehightraveller/istockphoto: 22b. Michael Pitts/Nature PL: 19b. Jason Patrick Ross/Shutterstock: 21t. Tui de Roy/Nature PL: 3t, 11b, 23t. SoopySue/istockphoto: 11t. Kuttelvaserova Stuchelova/Shutterstock: front cover. StuPorts/istockphoto: 15b. TomekD76/istockphoto: 3b, 21b. Ann & Steve Toon/Nature PL: 7t. Wild Wonders of Europe/Zanki/Nature PL: 2t, 17t. worldwildlifewonders/Shutterstock: 22t.

CONTENTS

The animal kingdom

Scientists sort all living things on Earth into five huge groups called kingdoms. All the animals belong in the animal kingdom.

The animal kingdom is divided into two very large groups. The invertebrates are animals without a backbone and the vertebrates are animals with a backbone.

INVERTEBRATES

ANIMAL KINGDOM

Then we divide the vertebrates up again, into five large groups: fish, amphibians, reptiles, birds and mammals.

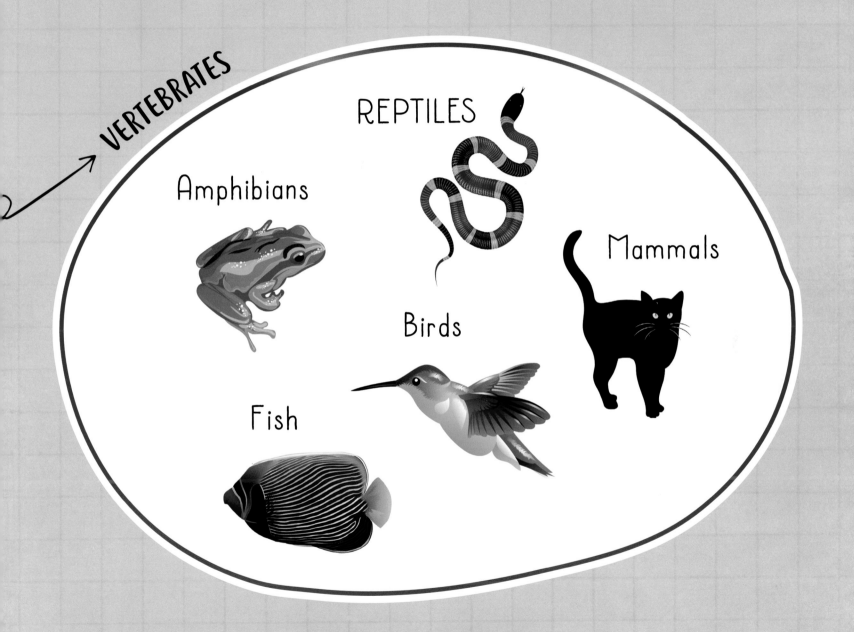

VERTEBRATES

REPTILES

Amphibians

Mammals

Birds

Fish

Read on to find out what makes an animal a reptile.

Reptiles have scaly skin

Reptiles have dry skin covered with scales or horny plates to protect their bodies. The skin is watertight.

Panther chameleon

Which other animals have scales on their skin?

Many reptiles need to shed their skin, or moult, in order to grow. Snakes do this all at once.

Adder's old skin

Most lizards shed their skin a bit at a time.

Patch of old skin

7

Reptiles have four legs, flippers or none

Lots of reptiles have four legs. Alligators walk on four legs and use their long tail to swim fast.

Tortoises have four short legs with long claws for digging burrows.

Red-footed tortoise

Sea turtles have flippers for swimming.

Snakes have no legs but can move fast on land or in water.

Banded sea snake

Reptiles are cold-blooded

Reptiles are cold-blooded – they cannot keep themselves warmer or cooler than the air around them.

This Nile monitor lizard is warming up on a hot rock. Once it is warm it will have the energy to move.

Marine iguanas bask on a rock.

Then they drop into the cold sea to find seaweed and algae to eat.

Which other animals are cold-blooded?

Reptiles live on land and in water

Deserts are home to many different types of lizard. The shovel snouted lizard stops its feet from burning on hot sand by lifting them up, two at a time.

Eastern painted turtles

These freshwater turtles are warming up on a log but can sleep underwater for hours.

Tropical rainforests are home to lots of different snakes.

Madagascar tree boa

All reptiles have lungs and breathe air. How do you breathe?

Many reptiles eat other animals

All snakes hunt animals to eat. Snakes have mouths that stretch to swallow animals whole.

Bush viper

Veiled chameleon

Tortoises and some lizards only eat plants.

A chameleon shoots out its sticky tongue to catch an insect.

Nile crocodiles eat fish but will grab any animal that comes close to them.

Most reptiles lay eggs

Most reptiles find a safe, warm place to lay their eggs and then leave them to hatch.

Female sea turtles dig a nest, lay their eggs, cover them up and return to the sea.

Baby sea turtle

A baby reptile grows inside its leathery or rubbery egg until it is ready to hatch.

Some snakes and lizards protect their eggs until they hatch.

A few reptiles give birth to live young.

Five-lined skink

Baby reptiles look like their parents

Can you guess what these babies are?
(The answer is on page 24.)

Mother crocodiles, alligators and caimans protect their eggs and young. This mother caiman is carrying her baby down to the river.

Most reptile babies can look after themselves as soon as they hatch.

Komodo dragon babies

Which other animals lay eggs?

Reptiles use their senses

Reptiles use their senses to find food and keep safe from danger. Most geckos hunt at night and can see in colour, even in the dark.

Giant leaf-tailed gecko

How well can you see in the dark?

Snakes and some types of lizard use their tongues to smell the air.

A chameleon can swivel its eyes in different directions to hunt for insects to eat.

Reptiles large and small

The largest reptile on Earth today is the Australian saltwater crocodile.

The tiny dwarf chameleon is one of the smallest reptiles. It lives in Madagascar.

The giant tortoise can live to 150 years old.

Tuatara lived on Earth before the time of the dinosaurs. They still live in New Zealand.

There are over 9,000 species of reptile worldwide.

Which of these animals is NOT a reptile?

Snake Crocodile Frog Tortoise Turtle

Answer: see the bottom of the page

Glossary

algae Very simple plants that live in water.

amphibian An animal that can live both on land and in water.

backbone A row of small bones that are connected together to form the spine.

bask To lie or sit in a warm place.

burrow An underground tunnel or hole.

caiman A reptile in the crocodile family.

freshwater Found in fresh water, not salty seawater.

hatch To come out of an egg.

horny plates Thick plates of hard material covering the body of some reptiles.

insect An animal with six legs and a body divided into three parts.

scales Thin plates of hard material that cover the body of some reptiles and fish.

skink A type of lizard with short legs.

species A kind of living thing, such as a red-footed tortoise.

tropical rainforest Thick forest that grows in warm parts of the world where it rains a lot.

tuatara A lizard-like reptile found only in New Zealand.

watertight Does not allow water to get in or out.

Answer to question on page 18: Caimans

Answer to question above: Frog – it is an amphibian